Cryptocurrency

Investing, Trading & Mining in Blockchain, Bitcoin & Altcoins

By

Jack Monroe

Disclaimer Notice

Please note the information contained within this document is for educational and entertainment purposes only. No warranties of any kind are expressed or implied. Readers acknowledge that the author is not engaging in the rendering of legal, financial, medical or professional advice. Please consult a licensed professional before attempting any techniques outlined in this book.

By reading this document, the reader agrees that under no circumstances are is the author responsible for any losses, direct or indirect, which are incurred as a result of the use of information contained within this document, including, but not limited to, —errors, omissions, or inaccuracies.

Contents

Introduction

Welcome to the world of cryptocurrency. It's a complicated world, not everyone understands it but one thing I can assure you of is this – it is not just a fad. I will attempt to guide you through the most important aspects of cryptocurrency – what it is, what a blockchain is, tips on investing and a look at some of the most popular cryptocurrencies in existence today.

Cryptocurrencies are more than just a passing phase, they are one of the biggest global phenomenon. While they may still be seen as a little bit geeky and not really understood, or perhaps misunderstood, by many people, the financial sector, and the governments, not to mention many corporations are well aware of their existence and of the threat they pose to them.

Right now, you will struggle to find any major accounting companies, banks, governments or software companies that have not carried out extensive research on cryptocurrencies, that haven't published some kind of paper on it or even started their own blockchain project. But beyond all of this, beyond everything you see in the media, most of us, even the big boys in government and finance, have very little knowledge about cryptocurrencies, failing to grasp even the most basics of concepts.

So, this book is all about cryptocurrencies, where they came from, what they are and everything else that you need to know about them. By the time you get to the end, you will be more knowledgeable and will be better placed to make decisions about whether you should or shouldn't invest any time and money into them.

Chapter 1: Crypto 101

So, what exactly is a cryptocurrency? To answer that, we must go back to 2008. Not many people realize that today's cryptocurrencies came about as a side-product of the Bitcoin. Satoshi Nakamoto released a white paper in 2008 detailing a system by which people would be able to make secure and fast transactions, a peer-to-peer (P2P) electronic cash system. It was never his intention to create any kind of currency, he just wanted to create something that so many had failed at before.

Bitcoin was actually released in 2009 as a peer-to-peer (P2P) network designed to stop the problem of double-spending. It is a decentralized system that has no central authority and no server, a complete success on the back of so many failures in the 1990's. After more than 10 years of failed systems based on the trusted third-party, the idea was written off and, after seeing all of this, Satoshi attempted to build their trusted cash system without the need for a central authority, something like the P2P networks many of us use for file sharing but for transactions instead.

It was this decision that prompted the development of cryptocurrency. These are the missing pieces that were needed for digital cash to succeed and once you understand why you will understand cryptocurrency.

In order for digital cash systems to work, you will require a payment network. That payment network needs to have accounts and balances along with transactions. That's the easy bit. Every payment network has got one big problem that they need to solve – to stop double-spending. Double spending is, as you would expect, when a person spends the same cash twice. With most payment networks, a central server is used to keep records of balances but with digital cash, there is no server.

This is where the blockchain comes in where the network peers do their job. Every computer that is linked to the digital cash network is called a peer or a node. Each one of these has an identical copy of the transactions ledger - the blockchain. Each time a transaction is made, this ledger is checked – partly to see if the transaction is a double-spend and partly to confirm that it is a legitimate transaction.

If just one of these balances is disagreed on by the network peers, the entire system will break. For a digital cash system to work it must have complete consensus across the peers. Again, normally a central authority would be needed to declare and record the correct balances, but digital cash doesn't have this central authority. That led many to believe that consensus was impossible, that digital cash could never succeed without a central authority.

Satoshi Nakamoto proved everyone wrong, producing a system that worked, a system where consensus was achieved without the central authority. Part of his solution is the cryptocurrency, and this is the bit that has got the entire world into a tizzy.

So, what are these cryptocurrencies? If you clear away everything that surrounds a cryptocurrency, strip it back to its bare bones, you will find that it is nothing more than a limited set of entries stored in a database that can't be changed with a set of specific conditions being fulfilled.

Think about this in terms of the cash in your bank

account – that is nothing more than a series of entries, stored in a database, that require specific conditions to be fulfilled before being changed. All money, be it physical or digital, is nothing more than a verified entry in a database that consists of accounts and balances, as well as transactions.

So, why should you use cryptocurrency? That's a really good question and the answer to it is really quite simple. Cryptocurrencies are a huge step in the direction of a global trade that we can all get involved in. If you were to push aside cryptocurrencies as nothing more than a fad to be ignored, it would be akin to pushing aside the idea of the internet and HTTP back in the 1990s. If you can understand the technology then you can understand how cryptocurrencies are going to shape our future, the benefits they bring.

The Benefits of Cryptocurrency

- Borderless transactions. Send money anywhere in the world to anybody in an instant, no hefty fees, and no middleman to worry about
- Everyone can be included in the financial system; it won't just be limited to those who can access can use modern-day banking
- Cryptocurrencies provide us with a basis for building on the blockchain to change how we see and interact with money
- We can use the significant computing power that is generated in mining cryptocurrencies to create decentralized networks for applications that work on top of a blockchain – networks like Ethereum who target the framework for building applications and running them rather than the money or currency aspect.

Chapter 2: Popular Cryptocurrencies

There are more than 1000 active cryptocurrencies available today and, while some of them will go nowhere, others have become very important ones, like Bitcoin, Ethereum, and Litecoin. So, how do these three compare with one another? Let's take a closer look.

Bitcoin

Bitcoin has now been given the honor of being adopted as a legitimate currency by Japan and what this means is that, in time, Japanese citizens will be able to use Bitcoin to pay off their tax bills. Bitcoin saw a significant surge upwards in price in August of 2017 and part of this is down to the news from Japan and partly because many people believed that, once the price of a Bitcoin reached $3000, the bubble would burst. It didn't, and it continues to rise.

Lastly, Bitcoin has seen an increase in amateur investors and that helped the price surge. However, it is these amateur investors that will be the first to bottle it and pull out when things start to look a bit rough and this is what will cause the bubble to finally burst where it may not have done if the price had risen more smoothly. It is worth remembering that the price of Bitcoin, and that of all cryptocurrencies, is somewhat volatile and what might look a significant drop doesn't really mean all that much – so far, where the price has risen significantly and then dropped, it has settled and gone back up again.

Right now, Bitcoin transaction times stand at around 10 minutes and this is expected to fall significantly given time. This, in turn, will increase how and where Bitcoin is used, and, of all the current cryptocurrencies, it is the one that will likely be adopted as a mainstream currency. Bitcoin will allow people to put their wealth away where governments and banks do not get a look-in.

Ethereum

Unlike Bitcoin, which is set at 21 million coins, there is no hard cap to Ethereum and this means that the early miners don't get the advantage of holding all the power. And, with the transaction time being incredibly fast, less than a minute, it also means it has a chance of being in use as legitimate currency at some point in the future, a time when you will be able to walk into a physical store and use Ethereum tokens to make purchases. So, does that make Ethereum something the economy will struggle to handle or is it just going to be another place for people to chuck all their money before it crashes and burns?

Right now, that question isn't going to go anywhere so perhaps a better question would be this – what will happen when the ICO (initial Coin Offering) cryptocurrencies, like Ethereum tokens, get to zero? Many people have invested in Ethereum because they believe that it is going to be the next best thing. With Ethereum, you are not getting a cryptocurrency that you can make purchases with, at least not yet. What you are getting is fuel, a fuel that developers have to pay to develop and run their applications on the Ethereum blockchain. Applications like smart contracts, which we will discuss a bit later on. So, what will happen to Ethereum, one of the most programmable of all cryptocurrencies, as opposed to the completely unprogrammable Bitcoin, when Ethereum tokens are worthless, which could happen?

One argument is that Litecoin is a better bet than Ethereum, it fills more of a gap or a need. Yet there is also the very high chance that, while some countries may not adopt Bitcoin as a legitimate currency, they may well adopt Ethereum. We already know that the Bitcoin has been a godsend for Africa and the Middle East, simply because workers cannot trust their banks, yet it is highly unlikely that these governments are going to adopt any cryptocurrency, not even a token like Ethereum, as a mainstream currency. Yet, when you look at a country like Greece, and you consider the severe financial situation the Greeks are in, you could wonder if perhaps they would do better to adopt Ethereum as a second form of currency, giving their people a bit more control over their own money, more freedom than the failing banks allow them. The Greek government is not going to worry too much about any reprisal from the banks if they did do this and the tax collectors have got the smarts to realize that they can look at how Ethereum is being used to see if anyone is using it as a tax dodge.

Litecoin

One of the biggest selling points to Litecoin is in the

speed of the transactions, which is one of the reasons why Litecoin was developed – to provide an alternative to Bitcoin. But, as time goes on, transaction times for both Ethereum and Bitcoin are going to get faster so what will happen to Litecoin when its selling point is gone? That really is anyone's guess, but it wouldn't do to underestimate Litecoin because, time and again, we've seen the underdog, the loser in the race turning up trumps and pushing past all the others.

Litecoin is a friendly, lighter version of the Bitcoin and it is more scalable, that cannot be denied. But, being so close to Bitcoin, it could be killed off by the same things, like quantum computing, that could kill off Bitcoin. Yet, if we want to talk about these things then we could still say that Bitcoin could become mainstream simply because a US bank got hit by a bomb from North Korea Litecoin has got to find its own place in the market, its own need and then it must be able to meet that need. Bitcoin is meeting the needs of the Middle Eastern and the African people who can't trust their banks, so Litecoin, if it cannot find that need, logic dictates it will die.

Investment Terms

So, which would you invest your money in? All three of these cryptocurrencies are good investments. Litecoin and Bitcoin are both primarily digital currencies while Ethereum is the best for distributed applications. Bitcoin and Litecoin have the main purpose of transferring value while Ethereum offers the best possibilities for giving us value via operations that happen on all the computers within the network, through their smart contracts. So, in terms of investment:

- **Ethereum** – lots of applications and a good technology that has a great future. Ethereum has been on a gradual rise this year, with a few ups and downs, but its value has increased overall, and this uptrend is expected to continue.

- **Litecoin** – the 5th biggest cryptocurrency using the blockchain technology, Litecoin prices have shot up by around 1400% this year alone. Potentially, it can offer far more value than Bitcoin and, like Bitcoin, it is decentralized, it can be mined, and it will operate on a global basis. Transaction times are around 2 minutes, about 5 times faster than Bitcoin and this may well be a determining factor in its future.

Bitcoin – obviously the first and the most popular of all cryptocurrencies, Bitcoin is a global force. While some say it will not rice past the prices of ETH or LTC next year, there are others that believe it will reach the heady heights of $50,000 or even $100,000 per coin.

Chapter 3: Cryptocurrency Mining

Crypto coin mining is a race and the best placed to win are the early adopters. Bitcoin mining used to be the most popular but not anymore. With so many more cryptocurrencies about, most of them costing less to mine than Bitcoin. More about that later; for now, the three cryptocurrencies that provide the best benefit to miners for the cost they incur are Litecoin, Feathercoin and Dogecoin. Take Litecoin, for example; with consumer level hardware from mining, you could earn up to $10 per day which doesn't sound much but is far more than Bitcoin. Likewise, Feathercoin and Dogecoin aren't quite so profitable but are fast becoming popular.

Is Crypto Coin Mining Worth it?

If you use crypto coin mining as something more of a hobby then yes, you can earn a couple of dollars per day doing it. Expect to pay around $1000 for hardware and you could recoup that money in a year or two. Treat it as a second income and it's highly unlikely to succeed and is certainly not a reliable income method for many. You can only make significant gains in crypto coin mining if you are prepared to invest between $3,000 and $5,000 in hardware; this could bring you a reward of upwards of $50 a day.

At some point, we may expect the value of all three of these cryptocurrencies to jump and, at that point, you have the potential to find yourself hoarding thousands of dollars in digital currency, but this is not a given and you shouldn't expect to become a crypto coin millionaire! So, if you decide to give mining a go, only think of it as a hobby and only expect a small return on it.

If your goal is to get yourself a significant amount of second income, then use your cash to buy crypto coins – don't mine them – and put them away with the hope that they will rise in value.

How Does Crypto Coin Mining Work?

This is for the beginners among you who don't want to go over $1000 in hardware costs up front and we are looking mining Litecoin, Dogecoin, and Feathercoin. Mining is done to accomplish these 3 things:

- To provide the network with book-keeping services. Mining is nothing more than computer accounting, done 24/7, to verify transactions
- Get some kind of reward for your work with payment in fractions of the coin every few days
- Keeping your costs down, and that includes electricity costs as well as hardware

What you need to mine:

To mine these 3 crypto coins, you will need 10 things:

1. A coin wallet which is a private database you can get for free. A wallet is a container with password protection that you keep your coins in and is where your transactions are held. (Check my free guide to set up a coin wallet)
2. Mining software that has stratum and cgminer packages in it – this is free
3. Mining pool membership. A pool is a group of miners that combine their computing power to increase the stability of their income and profitability

4. Exchange membership. You need an account at an online exchange where digital currency can be changed for fist currency (the money your country uses) and vice versa.

5. An internet connection that is reliable, preferably at least 2 MB/S or higher

6. A cool and air-conditioned area to set your hardware up in

7. A computer, either desktop or custom-built for mining. You can use your existing one but, once you begin mining, you will not be able to use it for anything else so a dedicated one is best. Forget about using laptops, handheld devices or gaming devices because they simply are not effective enough for an income to be generated.

8. An ATI GPU (graphics processing unit) or an ASIC chip (special processing device). These will cost anywhere between $90 for a used one and $3000 for a new one and these are the workhorses, the power behind the mining and accounting.

9. A standard fan that blows cool air over your setup. Mining has the potential to create significant amounts of heat and keeping your hardware cool is critical

10. Curiosity. You really do need to have a good appetite for learning as the mining environment and technology is constantly changing and being optimized. The best miners will spend several hours every week just trying to earn new ways to optimize their mining performance and potential for profit.

What about Bitcoin Mining?

If you had been one of the early adopters back in 2009, by now you would have earned several thousands of dollars.

However, you could also have lost it all. Right now, Bitcoin mining is done only by the larger-scale operations and the reason for this is that the mathematical algorithms that need to be solved have become significantly more difficult over the years, way beyond what any regular person could possibly expect to achieve with a home setup. The current cost of purchasing and maintaining the hardware required now would now be way over what a small-scale miner could possibly justify spending and it would take years for any profit to be realized, if ever.

So, unless you have many thousands of dollars to spend on industrial-grade hardware and airconditioned offices or warehouses to hold the equipment, there won't be any profit in it. You would be better off using that money to purchase Bitcoins and holding them until the value rises again.

Litecoin, Feathercoin, and Dogecoin are all possibilities for small-scale miners but, should you decide that you do want to have a go at mining Bitcoin, here's what you will need:

- Graphics cards
- Processor
- Power supply
- Cables
- Memory
- Fans

That might not look like an impressive list, but you would need to spend anywhere between $2,000 and $4000 dollars and that doesn't take into account the cost of powering the system and maintaining it.

Chapter 4: What is Blockchain Technology?

Many people often get a little confused when they try to understand blockchain technology, but it really isn't as complicated as it all seems. In fact, the basic concept of the blockchain is very simple. We have data that we do not want to be tampered with, copied or accessed in any other way but we all know that the internet isn't quite as safe as we perhaps think it should be. Hacking attacks are an almost daily occurrence now and it's getting harder to safeguard any data. With the blockchain, we get something that doesn't change, a database that cannot be tampered with and where transactions can only happen if they have followed the rules.

If you read the Bitcoin white paper from Satoshi Nakamoto, then you will know that it talks about how to mine data into blocks, and then chain the blocks together using a hash, which is a time-stamped link, across a network of nodes that is decentralized. Each node or computer on the network will then verify the transaction. One innovation that comes out of the white paper, a key point, is something called PoW, or Proof of Work. This model is used to create the trustless distributed consensus and is also the solution that Nakamoto found to solving double-spend for good.

Although the system is called "trustless" it shouldn't be taken to mean that it can't be trusted because it means the exact opposite. The blockchain will verify every single transaction through the PoW model and this means that there is no need for trust between any of the participants in the transaction. This proof of work comes from the miners, each one generating the PoW as they hash the blocks together and verify each transaction that is then put onto the ledger.

Perhaps a better explanation of the blockchain would be this – digital currency is not saved somewhere in a file. Instead, it is a series of transactions listed on a ledger or a spreadsheet with a copy stored on millions of different computers. Each computer verifies and approves the transactions and stores them permanently on the ledger, a ledger we now as the blockchain. The blockchain is distributed among all the computers which means there isn't any centralized database. Anyone can see it because it lives on that network and it is fully encrypted, using a combination of public and private keys to maintain full security.

It is, however, worth keeping in mind that nothing is completely protected from hacking, especially when it hasn't been used as intended. The reason why the security on the blockchain works is partly because of the encryption and partly because it is a decentralized system. You could point out to me that there have already been some major hacks on the blockchain and millions of Bitcoins and Ethereum tokens already stolen but there is a good reason for that. The two biggest are Mt. Gox (2014) and Bitfinex (2016) and the reason they were hacked and cleaned out was down to them attempting to centralize the system. The DAO hack on Ethereum is another famous one and that was traced back to a number of exploits in some of the smart contracts that were written on a blockchain that was already well established. And the biggest Ethereum exchange in South Korea was hacked and the ICO of an Israeli startup was stolen when their website got hacked.

Every single one of these issues happened because there were weaknesses in the systems that were connected to the blockchain – none of them came from the blockchain itself. The security and the encryption that underlies the blockchain is incredibly sound and cannot be hacked into or broken without a serious amount of computing power and the agreement of every computer on the network.

Ok, so we know how the blockchain functions and we know that it is secure but what about the way the blocks connect to one another? Why does the blockchain strengthen s it gets longer and where does the issue of immutability come into the equation?

The real heartbeat of the blockchain network is in the elf-checking system. Every 10 minutes, transactions are checked, verified, agreed and then stored in a block and this gets linked to the block before it, providing a chain. In order for a block to be valid, it must link to the one before it and the entire structure puts a permanent time stamp on everything, storing exchanges of value which stops anyone from tampering with and changing anything on the ledger. This ledger is distributed among all the nodes on the network, creating a network consensus of all transactions that have ever happened on the blockchain.

This digital ledger is also programmable to record pretty much anything of value, such as marriage licenses, birth certificates, death certificates, deeds, ownership titles, degrees, accounts, medical records, provenance and so on – anything that may be expressed in a code.

Immutability is a more crucial part of the equation when you are attempting to understand the blockchain. Once created, an object that can never be altered has got infinite value in today's digital world. The more nodes there for the blockchain to be distributed over, the stronger it is and the more trusted it is. Think of it as verification of verification and on to infinity. The network effect is what creates the strength in the immutability factor, especially with Bitcoin. To create a new digital asset, it costs practically nothing, so you need to be able to demonstrate a not inconsiderable amount of value to overcome that network effect if you wanted to tempt people away from the Bitcoin blockchain – a blockchain that is trusted and has the highest level of security, not to mention its proven track record.

That's the Bitcoin blockchain but what about Ethereum? What about these smart contracts we keep hearing about?

Smart Contracts

This is where the real value of the blockchain comes into play. Because it is decentralized, a system between permitted parties, there isn't any need for middlemen which saves time and eliminates conflict. Blockchains do have their issues but they are much faster, much cheaper and definitely more secure than the traditional system we have always relied on and this is why the governments and banks are gradually turning to them.

Back in 1994, it was realized by a cryptographer and legal scholar called Nick Szabo that decentralized ledgers could be used for creating smart contracts. These were otherwise known as self-executing contracts, digital contracts or blockchain contracts. Using this format, a contract could be turned into code and stored on the system, being replicated and then supervised by the network of nodes responsible for running the blockchain. The result of this would be ledger feedback like the transfer of money and receipt of services or goods.

What are Smart Contracts?

A smart contract lets you exchange money, shares, property or anything of value in a way that is transparent, free of conflict and without the need for a middleman. Think of the technology behind the smart contract as being like that of a vending machine. The normal way to draw up a contract would be to have it done by a notary or a lawyer, pay your money and then wait while the contract is drawn up. With the smart contract, you pop a coin into the vending machine (the ledger) and the goods or service that you paid for immediately lands in your account. The contract will include all the rules and the penalties of a traditional contract but also automatically enforces those rules and penalties.

Vitalik Buterin is responsible for the development of Ethereum and he explained it by saying that your currency or asset is put into a program and that program will run the code. At a point, the code will validate a given condition automatically and will determine whether the asset or currency should go to the person purchasing it or back to the person selling it. The document is replicated on the decentralized ledger, providing the required security and immutability. Let me try to explain that a bit better.

Let's say that I am renting you a house through the blockchain and you are paying for it in cryptocurrency. You get the receipt for your payment and this will be held inside the virtual contract between us. In return for your payment, I provide you with a digital key by a date specified in the contract.

If I don't get your payment by the specified date, I don't send the key. If you do send your payment and I don't send you the key by the specified date, you are automatically given a full refund. If I send you the ley before the specified date, that and the payment you sent will automatically be held until the specified date, at which point the key is released to you and the payment to me.

This is a faultless system that works on the premise of If-Then and it has literally hundreds of witnesses. Each contract has an automatic cancellation date built into it and neither you nor I can tamper with the code without the other knowing because both of us would be alerted at the same time.

The smart contract can be used for all sorts of things, from financial derivatives to breach contracts, from insurance premiums to property law, financial services, crowdfunding agreements, credit endorsement and legal processes, to name just a few.

Chapter 5: Cryptocurrency Forks

One thing that you may have heard a fair bit about recently, in terms of cryptocurrencies, is 'forks'. Not a table fork though. On the blockchain, a fork happens when participants are unable to agree on some common rules. The most basic way of explaining it is to say that a fork happens when the blockchain splits, creating two paths ahead. It may happen in regard to the transaction history on the network or because of a new rule in determining the validity of a transaction. A result is that all the participants must decide which choice they are going to support.

There are quite a few different kinds of fork and they are still pretty new. Some will resolve themselves, but others can cause a permanent split in the community, resulting in the creation of two blockchain histories and two currencies. There is also some confusion about the types of forks, how they are activated and what risks are posed by them.

The Basics

Before we look at the classifications of forks, you should be aware that Bitcoin forks are quite a regular occurrence. As a byproduct of the distributed consensus system, a fork can happen when two miners come to a block at virtually the same time. The ambiguity that surrounds it is solved by adding subsequent blocks to one, turning it into the longer chain and orphaning the other one, at which point it is abandoned.

However, forks are also deliberately introduced into the network and this happens when developers want to change the rules used by the software in determining the validity of a transaction. If a block has got invalid transactions in it, the entire block is ignored and the miner who originally found the block will lose his potential reward. Because of that, miners only want to mine the valid blocks and build the longer chains.

These are the most common forks you will hear about:

Hard Fork

A hard fork is, essentially, an upgrade to the software that brings new rules in that are not compatible with the older version of the software. If for example, a rule was introduced that expanded the block size from 1MB to 2MB, a hard fork would be needed. Any node that continues running the older software will see any block mined under the new rules as invalid, so all of the nodes would need to upgrade their software to the new rules, so all blocks mined would be valid.

The problem arises when not all nodes agree – some will want to stay with the old rules while others will want the new rules. One of the best case studies of this is the DAO Ethereum fork – we now have Ethereum and Ethereum Classic, both with different rules and with different currencies.

Soft Fork

By contrast, a soft fork is a change that is classed as being backward compatible. For example, instead of the 1MB block size, it's suggested to cut it down to 500KB. Any node that has not been upgraded will still be able to see the transactions as being valid but, should they mine the blocks, these blocks would be rejected as invalid by the upgraded nodes.

The problems arise when a soft fork only gets the support of a minority of the network hash power, turning it into potentially the shortest blockchain and risking it being abandoned. The only other way is for it to turn to a hard fork and split off.

Soft forks are the most common option for upgrading the Bitcoin blockchain because they have a lower risk factor of splitting the community and the network. 2 examples from the past are P2SH, which changed the way the Bitcoin address was formatted, and BIP66, which was to do with the way signatures are validated.

User-Activated Soft Fork

A UASF or user activated soft fork is somewhat controversial and deals with the addition of a blockchain upgrade that doesn't have direct support form those who provide the hashing power. The idea behind it is that, rather than waiting for a certain level of support from the mining pools, the power is given to the exchanges, the wallets and the businesses who run full nodes.

For the change to be permanently written into code, it would need to have the support of the majority of the big exchanges and this needs to be public support, the software has a future activation date, and, with the majority agreement, the software is installed on those nodes that want to be involved in the fork.

The problems arise because this type of fork needs a longer lead time than soft forks that are triggered by hashing power. It could take up to a year, perhaps more, to get the code written and ensure that everyone is ready for it. And, if that majority don't fall into line and the new rules don't get activated, they could take their hash power and split the network apart with it.

So far, this is only a theoretical idea and has not yet been implemented.

Chapter 6: Wallets and Exchanges

One commonly asked question revolves around where to store your cryptocurrency. There are those that want to store it in the exchange they use to purchase it through and others advocate the use of a wallet. We'll look at both of these now.

What is a Cryptocurrency Exchange?

A cryptocurrency exchange is a website where you buy and sell cryptocurrencies or trade them for fiat or other digital currencies. If you are looking to become a professional trader, with access to all the tools you need for trading then you will be using an exchange, and you will be required to open an account and verify who you are. This will take a few days because you will need to upload some form of photographic ID for verification purposes and you will also need to verify your payment method/s. If you are only interested in making the odd trade, then you can use a trading platform that doesn't need you to open the account first. Before you open an exchange account, shop around. Only use one that is reputable and check which fiat currencies they accept – not all will accept your currency. Also check on the trade prices because they can vary quite wildly between exchanges, as can any fees payable.

Should you store your cryptocurrency on the exchange? That is a good question. In some cases, it is a good idea to store coins on the exchange because it will allow for quick trading. However, you should only keep a small amount in there; not the whole lot because there is always a chance that the exchange could be hacked, or the owners decide to hut up shop and disappear, taking your coin with them. Recently, the

BTC-e exchange was closed down because the exchange owner got arrested for money laundering and all money contained in the exchange passed to the FBI. While the owners of those coins may well get them back, they are likely to wait until the FBI has finished their investigations. So, what about a wallet?

What are Cryptocurrency Wallets?

A cryptocurrency wallet is a piece of software that is used for the storage of your public and private keys. The public key is your cryptocurrency address, and this is what every transaction you make is linked to. The private key is your password – this cannot be regenerated so keep it safe; if you lose it or it is stolen, you lose access to all the coins stored in your wallet. The wallet is a requirement for storage of Bitcoin and other cryptocurrencies and there are several to choose from:

- Online
- Cold storage
- Paper wallet

Online is self-explanatory; the wallet is kept online and is very easy to access but it is more open to hacking and your coins are under the control of a third-party – the wallet provider – and you are relying on them not to do a runner with your assets. Cold storage is secure as you are storing your wallet on a USB flash drive or another external storage device, but this must be connected to your PC before you can access it. Paper storage is a printed copy of your wallet keys and must be kept stored safely. Bear in mind that paper degrades over time and it can burn. You should have several copies of your paper wallet all stored in separate places.

How Do Wallets Work?

Cryptocurrency wallets are used by millions of people worldwide but not everyone truly understands how they work.

Don't mistake them for being anything like the physical wallet you carry now – digital wallets do not store currency in any form. It's fair to say that any cryptocurrency you purchase is not stored in any one location nor does it exist in any physical format. Instead, they are merely transaction records that are kept stored on the blockchain.

A wallet is a software program. Your keys are stored in it and they are used to interact with the blockchains so that you can keep an eye on your balances, send or receive cryptocurrency or carry out other transactions. When you are sent Bitcoin or another cryptocurrency, what happens is that they sign the ownership of the currency over to your wallet. To access and spend those coins, the private key that you have stored in your wallet has got to match the public key used to assign the currency to your wallet. If they match, all is well and the currency is yours. No coins are transferred, merely transaction records on the blockchain and the increase of the balance in your wallet.

So, where do you keep your cryptocurrency? Much depends on what you are going to do with it. If you intend to do a little day trading, then you need to keep some in your exchange account. If you are purchasing cryptocurrency for investment then the best option is to store it in a wallet, preferably offline or in paper format.

Obviously, what you do is your choice but be aware that your cryptocurrency will be much safer stored in a wallet than it will on the exchange. Weigh up your pros and cons, make the decision that suits you but just keep in mind that this is your hard-earned cash we are talking about – you want to keep it as safe as you possibly can.

Next, we are going to look at some tips on investment.

Chapter 7: Cryptocurrency Investing Basics

Investing and trading in cryptocurrency is not really any different to investing and trading in stocks and shares so here are some of the top tips on how to do it.

Important – Please do NOT treat this as professional advice for investment and trading in cryptocurrency. This is nothing more than advice that can help you but, if you want proper financial advice on investments, you should seek it from a proper financial adviser who specializes in cryptocurrency.

Let's start simple:

- Always use an exchange and not a broker – the fees will be cheaper
- Use limit orders when you buy and sell through exchanges; the fees will be lower
- Buy low and sell high. Watch the trends in price and wait for the highs to break before you buy.
- Don't put all your eggs in one basket. Spread your money around a bit and invest in two or three cryptocurrencies that have proven track records.
- Stick with Bitcoin, at least for the most part. Put some money into another altcoin but Bitcoin is a proven trade right now
- Don't trade everything. Hold some coins back in case of a dip in a currency and the chance to buy at a low price.
- Sometimes, a diverse portfolio and a diverse investing strategy can eat your profits up as often as it can hold off the losses. If you want to make huge profits all of the time you need to take some risks. Don't put it all into one coin in the hope that it is going to go up; if it does,

all's well; if not, you are a bit stuck until the price rises again.

- Don't jump at the first sign of the market going off. If you are working on a strategy stick to it. The market will occasionally go off the scale both in terms of rises and falls and, while it might make sense to buy or sell at that point, do not change your entire strategy without careful thought.

- Keep your eyes peeled for scams; there are a few around in the world of cryptocurrency. If a coin or an exchange or wallet doesn't have a good reputation, avoid it.

- Never invest any more money than you can comfortably afford to lose. While the price of Bitcoin looks great right now, that's only from a selling point of view. Buying at today's prices doesn't mean that you won't make a profit, but the chances are not as high as they used to.

- Take your profits. This is a conservative kind of strategy because, when you take your profits you make less than if you had just left them to ride. If your profits are good, remove them from the equation and wait for the prices to drop again.

- Set a stop order after you purchase your cryptocurrency. This will create a market order for when the price gets hit and while it means getting hit with fees and slippage it also means that your risk is easier to calculate.

- Keep an eye on the cryptocurrency news; has one country or another just banned the use of cryptocurrencies? Is a fork about to happen on Bitcoin or Ethereum? The news can give you a good idea of what is going to happen in the near future. When Bitcoin forks, all holders will get free coins. For example, when Bitcoin forked into Bitcoin cash, all Bitcoin holders were given 1 Bitcoin Cash for every Bitcoin that they held. The only downside is that you must be in the fork at the time of the capture date or the coins will not be given.

- Don't chase after free coins because a fork is not worth losing any money over. Bitcoin cash is worth a few hundred dollars while Bitcoin is worth several thousand If you end up losing hundreds to get one single Bitcoin cash coin, it really isn't worth it. Don't lose your cool and hold onto your strategy as far as you can.
- Don't bank everything on Bitcoin; there is a chance that one of the altcoins could overtake it in time. It may not always be the king of the castle.
- Learn the language. By that, I mean the common terms associated with cryptocurrency, like BTC (Bitcoin), ETH (Ether), ICO (initial Coin Offering), limits, exchanges, stops, wallets, forks, margin trades, and so on If you understand the terms, you will get on much better with trading.
- Know when the right time is to take a loss. It's no fun losing money but if for example, you are going short in Bitcoin and you never set a stop, it might be more sensible to take a loss and wait until the price is better.
- Always know what it is you are investing in and know what the risks are. Bitcoin is a highly speculative and incredibly volatile investment.
- Don't mistake Bitcoin for the blockchain; they are two completely different things.
- Fiat currency is not dead, and cryptocurrencies are not legal tender everywhere. The governments and the banks don't see cryptocurrencies in quite the same way that we do and getting too caught up in the craze can mean that you forget the governments don't necessarily

agree – right now, governments have power and it's very risky to bet against them.

- Understand the tax implications of cryptocurrency before you start trading. Right now, you pay your taxes in fiat currency. With cryptocurrency, you find yourself in a situation where you make a decent profit on paper but by the end of the year you are down in Bitcoin but didn't take the loss – you end up owing serious money in taxes, money you most likely don't have.

- The same is true of ICOS and Altcoins. On a good day, the altcoins generally follow Bitcoin, and, on a bad day, they are drained while BTC reaps the rewards. An ICO is a new altcoin and many are worth investing in – the gold doesn't flow out of them as well it does out of Bitcoin though so always be cautious when you decide to invest in ICOs and Altcoins.

- Track your cryptocurrency coin prices using a reputable source. One of the very best and most accurate is CoinMarketCap.

Investing and trading in cryptocurrency is a book all of its own; these are merely tips to guide you in the right direction and give you something to work on.

Chapter 8: FAQ

These are some of the top FAQs asked about cryptocurrencies:

1. **Can I buy cryptocurrency using PayPal?**

Some places will accept PayPal as a payment method although these are few and far between. Note that, with each of the sites, there are many steps involved signing in and creating your accounts. Although there are only a few places right now, notable Cryptonit, E-Coin, and Virwox, more and more are being added and transactions involving PayPal to Bitcoin are set to become a leading method because of the enhanced security and the credibility involved with each deal.

On the downside, using PayPal is risky to buy and sell Bitcoin or another cryptocurrency because of the risk of chargeback. Let's say that you opt to sell some Bitcoin using PayPal. The buyer sends you the money, you send the Bitcoin to the address provided and, a couple of days later, the buyer puts in a chargeback. They get their money back and the Bitcoin and you get left with nothing.

2. **What is a hash rate?**

Hash rate refers to the power and the speed of your mining rig or your card to carry out and complete an operation on the cryptocurrency code that you are mining. What it means is, the higher your hash rate of your video card or mining rig, the faster you can mine as the figures relate to speed and efficiency.

3. **How do you get money if it is all digital currency?**

Its quite simple you use fiat currency (the paper currency of your country) to exchange for a cryptocurrency at the exchange of your choice. If you are looking to purchase altcoins, you will need to purchase Bitcoin first, although some do accept Eth in payment as well. The Bitcoin is the digital version of the USD or the Euro – it is globally recognized and you can use exactly the same method to change your digital currency back to fiat currency. You will pay a fee for this though.

4. **How easy is it to make money in cryptocurrency?**

How long is a piece of string? There are several ways to make money; trading isn't the only way even if it is the most popular. However, while there have been stories of people who become overnight millionaires, don't expect it to happen to you, not at today's prices. You can trade cryptocurrency in much the same way as you do forex with the reminder that cryptocurrency trading is extremely volatile and is not regulated.

You could use your computer to mine for the cryptocurrency of your choice although you won't get a great deal this way and it could cost you way more than you could expect to make. Serious miners now have mining farms, rooms or warehouses full of equipment, all mining simultaneously and this is what has knocked the market out for Joe public.

Another way to make money is to loan what Bitcoin you own to a site that margin trades and make a little bit or you can get involved in other activities provided by technology companies that pay you in coins. Steemit is the most popular; similar to YouTube but you receive Bitcoin for putting content on the site. Don't expect to make a fortune though; your payment will be in fragments of a coin and it can take some time to build up one BTC!

5. **Is my money safe? What about if the digital asset bubble suddenly bursts?**

First, the bubble will not suddenly burst – you will get plenty of warning signs, you just need to know what you are looking for. The bubble bursting will hit traders very hard; if you choose to buy cryptocurrency and store it in a wallet, it won't hurt you so much because you can sit it out and wait for the prices to go back up – just don't lose your private key in the meantime!

The bubble being talked about right now is the incredible fluctuation of cash in the altcoin markets and this is happening because traders are throwing tons of cash at it in the hope of flipping a decent profit very quickly. The more money they throw in, the higher the price will go but this is artificial and not all of the altcoins are worth that kind of investment. In fact, some won't even get past investment and any money you put in will more than likely be lost.

6. **If cryptocurrency is that good, why aren't there more people involved?**

Because there are many people who don't trust something that they don't know much about or if something seems to be more geeky or techy, at least until it gets made mainstream. Think back to the early days of the internet, or of social media. It took ages for thee to be fully adopted and trusted by everyone and look now – everyone is connected to the net and social media accounts are amongst the largest in the world.

Cryptocurrency is exactly the same. When it first started, few people trusted it but now millions of people use it. We are all used to the rubbish returns we get from our banks and if someone says that you can make money hand over fist, you see it as too good to be true. The average bank or insurance return is 4-6% every year; a slightly savvier investor can make 9% of a portfolio, the better ones can hit 20%. In cryptocurrency, the returns could be as much as 20 to 50% every week. While that isn't a given it is certainly possible but not many people will trust in it – yet.

7. Isn't cryptocurrency just a Ponzi scheme?

Can't someone just take your money and run off with it? Yes and no. there are more than 1000 different coins out there and there are more being released every day. If you get confused by the thought of coins just consider them as apps that have a specific use. Some are good, some are complete rubbish. If you invest blindly in the rubbish ones, you are more likely to be caught out by a scam, so do your research before you put your money anywhere.

8. I haven't got a clue how to trade so how can I make money?

You can, because there are some reputable sites that will assist you in managing your portfolio, although they will charge you for this of course. Trading isn't for everyone; it can be hard, and it can take a lot of time. You need to understand what hedging your bets is all about, as well. The best way to start is to join a group that pools money and skills for a cause although these are mostly referral-based. To get in on them, you should join some chat groups and forums and start getting to know people. As always, never invest any more than you can comfortably afford to lose.

Cryptocurrency Glossary

#

51% Attack – when at least 51% of the network's computing power is controlled by a single person or group, they may carry out harmful transactions with malicious intent.

A-B

Address – An identifier made up of a string of random characters that allows blockchain transactions to happen between individuals or entities. Usually accompanied by a private key for accessing funds

Altcoin – Cryptocurrencies or tokens other than Bitcoin

Arbitrage – Taking full advantage of a price difference on one currency between two exchanges; usually mentioned in the context of the ETH price on US and Korean exchanges

ASIC – Acronym for Application Specific Integrated Circuit, these are made ONLY for mining and are cheaper in power cost than a standard mining rig. Can use Wi-Fi or Ethernet to connect to a network or computer

ATH - All-Time-High. The highest ever-price point of a cryptocurrency.

Bagholder – A person who is holding on to an Altcoin after a crash caused by a pump-and-dump scheme. May also refer to a person who is hanging on to a crypto coin whose value is dropping and has no real prospect for the future

Bearish – Commonly termed a Bear market in stocks, when the price is widely expected to fall

Bit – Commonly used to describe a sub-unit of the Bitcoin. 1 Bitcoin is equal to 1000 bits

Bitcoin – The very first open-source and decentralized cryptocurrency

Bitcoin Cash (BCH) – Created in 2017, BCH is a copy of Bitcoin blockchain with a higher block size (8MB as opposed to Bitcoin's 1MB); created after a fork

Block – A data record on the blockchain, more like a ledger page and containing details of transactions that are pending. Every 10 minutes or so, each block will be confirmed and added to the blockchain by miners

Block Explorer – A tool found online that lets you look through all Blockchain transactions and provides information such as the hash rate of the network

Block Height – How many blocks are connected on the blockchain

Block Reward - A reward or incentive to miners who can correctly calculate a block hash when mining. When transactions are verified, new coins get generated and the miner is given a percentage of these as his reward

Blockchain – The shared or distributed ledger where all cryptocurrency transactions get stored. Each block is affixed the next, creating a tamper-proof record of every single transaction ever made in a chain of blocks

Breakout – The point at which the market price of a digital asset or crypto coin goes past a resistance or support level that has already been defined

BTC – The official acronym for Bitcoin

Bullish – Described as a Bull market in stocks, this is when the price is widely expected to rise

Buy Wall – A buy order that is massive, stopping the market price from dropping until the buy order has been fully completed

Buying Pressure – This happens when a high percentage of traders are purchasing, an indicator that they are expecting an increase in market price

C-D

Central Ledger – A ledger that is being maintained by a centralized agency

Circulating Supply – The total number of a specific coin in circulation at any one time, and available for trading or spending

Cold Storage – A safer way of storing your cryptocurrency offline, stopping it from being lost through hacking. There are several ways of doing this but the most common include:

- Print a supplied QR code for a software wallet and keep it safe

- Take the files from the software wallet and store them on an external storage source, storing that away safe

- Use of a hardware wallet

Commodity Money – A currency whose value is a result of the commodity it is derived from

Confirmation – Successful hash of a transaction that is then added to the blockchain

Consensus – When all the network participants are in total agreement on transaction validity; this means that every copy of the blockchain is identical

Cryptocurrency – A digital currency produced by solving mathematical algorithms; decentralized and secured with cryptography so it cannot be manipulated or counterfeited.

Cryptographic Hash Function – A unique hash value of fixed size is produced by a cryptographic hash form transaction inputs of various sizes. An example of this is the SHA-256 algorithm

Cryptography – Math that is used by cryptocurrency to provide security on a high level. For example, with Bitcoin, the cryptography is used to make sure that the blockchain cannot be corrupted and the contents of a wallet cannot be spent by an unauthorized person

DAO – Acronym for Decentralized Autonomous Organization. This is venture capital fund that was based on Ethereum and, famously, got hacked in 2016. This resulted in a loss of around one-third of the funds and in a hard-fork happening not long after. This is referred to as one of the biggest problems to hit Ethereum to date

DaPP – Acronym for Decentralized Applications. These are open source applications that operate without human intervention. All data is kept on a blockchain, the incentive is by way of tokens and operates on a Proof of Value protocol

DASH – A cryptocurrency created in 2014, with a basis in the Bitcoin software but much more anonymous. Its features mean that transactions can never, ever be traced to any individual. Otherwise known as DarkCoin and XCoin.

DCA – Stands for Dollar Cost Averaging and used to reduce portfolio volatility. This is done by the spreading of buys and sells over a much longer time

DDoS – Acronym for Distributed Denial of Service. An attack of this kind involves one attacker and multiple computers and is designed to drain all the resources of the initial target. Some exchanges have been the victim of this kind of attack

Decentralized – No central agency, no central function and no central power which leads to there being no single PoF – point of failure. This leads to much higher security and trust

Difficulty – The ease or otherwise of the success of mining a transaction block

Digital Signature - Generated through the public key, this is code that is attached to each electronic document as a way of verifying both the identity of the sender and the contents of the document

Distributed Consensus – An agreement made collectively by the network computers that they will work in a P2P manner that is decentralized, with no need for any central agency to stop dishonesty on the network

Distributed Ledger – These are ledgers that store data on them across a network of computers or nodes. They do not have a currency and they may be private and permissioned

Distributed Network – A network where all the data and the processing power are distributed across the network nodes instead of in one central database

Double Spending – When money is spent twice – this cannot happen with cryptocurrency because of the verification process in place for each transaction

Dump – When a large amount of cryptocurrency is sold at the current market value by an individual or a group, resulting in the market price diving

E-F

EEA – Acronym for Enterprise Ethereum Alliance, which is a group of corporations and startups, with some very big names included, all trying to work out the best way of sing Ethereum

ERC-20 – An Ethereum token standard which is in place to ensure the tokens behave predictably. Because of this, they can easily be exchanged and will work with any ERC-20 compatible decentralized application. Most ICO tokens are compliant with the ERC-20 standard.

Ether (ETH) – The currency used on Ethereum to pay for tasks and transaction fees which are based on gas price and gas limit – these fees are paid in ETH

Ethereum – A decentralized platform built on the blockchain; used to run apps that use smart contracts and with the aim of eliminating issues that surround interference by third-parties, fraud, and censorship.

Ethereum Classic (ETC) – After the much-publicized DAO attack, the Ethereum blockchain split in a hard fork that was carried out to bring back the money that was stolen. ETC carries on as the original blockchain with the support of all those who believe that the blockchain should be entirely immutable and did not support the hard fork

EVM – Acronym for Ethereum Virtual Machine (EVM), which is a Turing Complete machine that will allow EVM Byte code to be executed by anyone. All Ethereum nodes run on this to ensure consensus is maintained across the blockchain

Exchange – A platform whereby users can exchange fiat currency for digital currency and vice versa

Fiat Currency – A currency that has little to no value and is produced by governments as and when needed or when the value needs to be tempered down. They do not have the backing of any commodity but are legal tender. This is the currency that you carry in your pocket today

FinCEN – A US Treasury agency, otherwise known as the Financial Crimes Enforcement Network. It was started as a way of protecting financial systems from illegal use and as a way of fighting back against money launderers. It is also responsible for collecting financial intelligence and analyzing it. This is the main US agency for the imposition of regulations on Bitcoin trading exchanges.

Flipping – A strategy in investing where a purchase is made with the sole purpose of selling it for a quick profit. As far as ICOs are concerned, flipping is the investment of the tokens before they hit the exchanges and then selling them on when they reach the secondary market

FOMO – Acronym for Fear of Missing Out. This is a reference to an apprehensive feeling of missing an investment opportunity that has the potential to be profitable which then leads to feelings of regret later down the line

Fork – A change to the cryptocurrency protocol that is not backward compatible. Forks tend to happen when a separate version of the blockchain is created by network nodes using a different protocol version. This second blockchain is not compatible with the original blockchain software, resulting in 2 that run side by side on different sections of the network.

FUD – Acronym for Fear, Uncertainty, and Doubt. It is when negative or false information is spread about, leading to a false perception of something

FUDster – A person responsible for spreading FUD

G-H

Gas – The amount of processing power that is used for processing transactions on the Ethereum network. The amount depends on the simplicity or complexity of the transaction with Smart Contracts among the highest in cost

Gas Limit – A term that describes how much a specific user is prepared to spend on any one transaction on the Ethereum network. There must be sufficient gas to execute the transaction, including all resources needed and, if there is any gas left over, it is returned back to the user

Gas Price – The amount in Eth for each of the gas units on any one transaction. The person who starts the transaction pays the required price and there is a priority system – high price transactions are executed first.

Genesis Block – The very first verified and processed block of any new blockchain, sometimes called Block 0 or, in some cases, Block 1

Going Long – Margin trade that will profit if the price goes up

Going Short – Margin trade that profits if the price goes down

Gwei – An Ether denomination, the one that gas prices tend to be measured in the most. 10,000,000,00 gwei is equal to 1 Ether

Hard Cap – The absolute maximum that an ICO will raise; once they get to the hard cap, they will stop raising funds

Hard Fork – A fork that will make any transactions that were invalid, valid and those that were valid will be rendered invalid. A hard fork requires that every node on the network is upgraded to use the latest software

Hard Wallet – A physical device that stores your cryptocurrency offline; general seen as the best and most secure storage facility

Hash Rate – The maximum hashes that are performed by a miner in a specified period, usually 1 second

Hash – Algorithm that converts variable data into fixed data or a shorter length

HODL – A meme that originally came about as a result of a spelling error in a Bitcoin forum, HODL is also referred to as "Hold on for Dear Life" or "Buy and Hold." It refers to a strategy of making a long-term investment irrespective of how volatile the market is.

Hybrid PoS/PoW -A consensus algorithm that uses the Proof of Stake and Proof of Work. This provides for a better balance between the voters and the miners and creates a system whereby the community is governed by both insiders and outsiders.

I-K

ICO – An Initial Coin Offering, much like the IPO or Initial Public Offering seen in stocks and shares. ICOs are set up to raise the required amount of money for a new project in cryptocurrency by offering a specific number of the coins for the public to buy. These coins are set at a base price and, over the long term, that price will go up or down depending on supply and demand.

IOTA (MIOTA) – A cryptocurrency and a distributed open source ledger that appeared in 2015, that is NOT based on the blockchain. Instead, it uses Tangle, a brand-new type of ledger. Features include no feed, better scalability and more security for transactions and it is almost entirely focused on IoT or the Internet of Things.

KYC – Acronym for Know Your Client and is also used to Know Your Customer. The guidelines for KYC state that all potential clients to any financial institution must be checked to make sure that they are real people and can provide identity verification. This is used by most of the big cryptocurrency exchanges

L-M

Lightning Network – a P2P system, off the blockchain and low-latency that allows for cryptocurrency micropayments to be made. Features include better scalability, instant payment, cheaper cost transactions and works cross-chan. There is no need for anyone to make a public transaction on the blockchain and smart contracts are used for enforcing the security of each transaction

Limit Order / Limit Buy / Limit Sell – These are orders that traders place for buying and selling when the price of a cryptocurrency gets to a specific point. They are much like the 'For Sale' signs that you see outside a house and are usually used in conjunction with Market Orders.

Liquidity – Describes the purchase and/or sale of a digital asset together with the process of the price staying consistent between each transaction

Litecoin (LTC) – Another cryptocurrency, created in 2011, by Charlie Lee who used to work for Google. Features include SegWit and use of the Lightning Network for low-cost faster processing times.

Margin Trading – Risking the crypto coins that you own to intensify your trades – this is NOT recommended for beginners, only for those who are very experienced in trading. It should also not be done on all exchanges, only certain ones

Market Cap – A cryptocurrency's total value, calculated through the multiplication of the total coin supply by the current market price of one unit

Market Capitalization – Total value of the supply in circulation of any give cryptocurrency

Market Order / Market Buy / Market Sell – Basic sale or purchase of a cryptocurrency at the current market price on an exchange. The market buy purchases the cryptocurrency at the cheapest available price and the market sell will sell at the highest available price

mBTC – A Bitcoin denomination worth about 0.001 BTC or one-thousandth of one bitcoin

MEW – Acronym for MyEtherWallet, a free online site for the generation of software wallets

Mining – The process of verifying transactions before putting them on the blockchain and is also how new coins are produced. Anyone with the right hardware and internet access can mine for cryptocurrency but the costs of power and the hardware, usually required on an industrial scale, will limit who can do it, specifically with Bitcoin

Mining Farm – A warehouse or large room loaded with mining rigs for multiple processing of the blockchain algorithms

Mining Pool – a group of miners who pool their computing and pricing power to mine. The payouts are lower but easier to get

Mining Rig - A specifically designed computer set up for mining, containing many top of the range GPUs for the maximum amount of processing power. Very expensive to purchase, these are usually out of the range of Joe Public and usually used by mining farms

Monero (XMR) – A cryptocurrency that came about in 2014, with a focus almost entirely on being scalable and private. It will run on multiple platforms, including Linux, Mac, and Windows, as well as Android. Transactions are not traceable to any specific person or true identity

Multisig – The official term for addresses that require multiple users to use public keys to seed a blockchain address. These are much more secure and less likely to be hacked into

N-O

NEM (XEM) – Reference to a cryptocurrency and a management platform for a range of assets, such as records of ownership, currency, supply chains, and so on Extra features includes multi-sig, message encryption and much more

NEO – A cryptocurrency that appeared in 2014 and is also the name of the first blockchain (open source) in China. Much like Ethereum, NEO facilitates smart contracts and DaPPs but suffers from issues with compatibility of coding languages.

Node - A computer on the blockchain network that holds and maintains a copy of the blockchain

Oracles – These provide smart contracts with data, bridging the gap between the blockchain and the real world.

P-Q

P2P– Acronym and common terms for Peer to Peer. This technology has long been used on the net for downloading and uploading files. In terms of cryptocurrency, it is referring to the decentralized transactions that take place between two or more parties without the interference of any third-party or regulatory body

Paper Wallet – Hard copy of your wallet with relevant information, including addresses and keys. Often used as a more secure way of storing cryptocurrency without using software solutions

Pre-Sale – A coin sale that happens before an ICO goes for public participation

Private Key – A random data string that provides access to the contents of a particular wallet. Much like a password, they must be kept safe because the loss of or theft of the key means losing access to your wallet forever.

Proof of Stake (PoS) – One of the blockchain algorithms, provides rewards for the solving of difficult puzzles or mathematical problems so that a distributed consensus may be achieved. Different to the PoW, transactions can be validated, and new blocks may be created based on the stake of an individual, such as the total number of coins that they own. Also uses less power than PoW.

Proof of Work (PoW) – Another blockchain algorithm that gives the reward to the person who solves the problem first. Miners are in competition with one another to solve mathematical problems so that the next block can be added to the chain. Because the service requester requires service time, cyber-attacks and spam attacks can be prevented.

PSP – Acronym for Payment Service Provider. These are agents for those places that will accept payments online

Public Address – The hash of the public key or blockchain address; they act the same way as an email address does, and can be made known publicly, unlike the private key.

Public Key – A string of alphanumeric characters that take on the job of a blockchain address when private keys are hashed with them for digital signing of any transaction. This key may be given to other individuals for the purpose of sending and receiving cryptocurrency

Pump – When an individual or group buys a lot of one type of coin at the current market price, pushing up the price

Pump and Dump Scheme – A scheme by which a project that doesn't have any real basis is hyped up to push up the price; the purchasers then sell as soon as the launch is made to make a tidy profit, thus potentially pushing the price back down again

QR code – Acronym for Quick Response code. A 2D image in a block that can be scanned on any device with a code reader (smartphone, tablet, etc.). The block image contains data and is sometimes used for bitcoin address ending. You will find one of these when you transfer your wallet offline.

R-S

Raiden Network – An Ethereum protocol change due to being implemented soon. This will also for transfers to be made at high speed, much like the Lightning Network from Bitcoin

Resistance Level – A point at which the price of a commodity or asset resists any more increases because of conditions in the market

Ripple (XRP) – A cryptocurrency that was based on OpenCoin and also the name of the payment platform (open source) where the currency may be transferred between users. The aim of Ripple is to enable a global payment system in real-time

ROI – Acronym for Return on Investment and refers to the percentage of profit made compared to the investment initially made. For example, 100% ROI would indicate that the investor has made 100% of their investment, doubling their money

Satoshi Nakamoto – The founder of Bitcoin, an unknown person or group of persons responsible for the Bitcoin protocol

Satoshi – A subunit of a bitcoin, 0.00000001 BTC is equal to 1 BTC

Scrypt – A cryptographic algorithm in use by Litecoin, much quicker than SHA-256 and uses less processing time and power

Segregated Witness (SegWit) – A process that increases the limit in a blockchain block size by moving the data for digital signatures to the end of each transaction to provide more capacity. Each transaction is split into two – the data and the signature

Sell Wall – A Massive sell order that stops the market price from increasing until the whole order has been completed

Selling Pressure – This happens when a high percentage of traders sell, an indication that they believe the price is going to drop

SEPA – Acronym for Single European Payment Area. This was set up as an EU integration payment system to facilitate payments in Euros between nations

SHA-256 – A cryptographic algorithm in use by some cryptocurrencies. Unlike Scrypt, Sha-256 uses more processing power and takes more time, thus making it more profitable for miners to form pools rather than attempting to mine alone

Sharding – A method by which network nodes can hold a part-copy of a blockchain instead the entire blockchain. This increases speed and performance

Shill – An individual who hypes up a cryptocurrency, over and above what it really is, because it is likely to be a scam

Smart Contracts – Usually run on the Ethereum platform, although others are now appearing, a Smart Contract is an automated system where two parties or more place their digital assets into a contract for later distribution. The contract will run without any downtime because it is automated, and it will only be completed when a specified event is triggered. An example would be Part A agreeing to pay Party B 100 BTC on receipt of an electronic key for a car hire agreement. The 100 BTC are placed into escrow and are only released on receipt of the key or if both the key and the BTC are placed into escrow at the same time, both will be released on a preset date.

Soft Cap – The absolute minimum that an ICO is looking to raise. If they do not reach that amount, the ICO will be canceled and any funds raised will be sent back to those who provided them

Soft Fork – Different from a hard fork, soft forks mean that transactions that were valid before the fork are invalid, the old network nodes will treat the new blocks ad being valid and, as such, the soft fork is backward compatible. Most network miners will need to upgrade to the new software for enforcement

Soft Wallet – Wallet software that stores cryptocurrencies online, on mobile devices or on computers

Solidity – The programming language used by Ethereum for smart contracts

Stable Coin – Cryptocurrency that has very low volatility and can be used for trading against the whole market

Support Level – A point at which market conditions stop decreases in price

T-V

TA – Acronym for Technical Analysis or Trend Analysis. This references the process by which current market charts are examined to try to predict whether the market is going to go up or down

Testnet – A blockchain developed for testing purposes so that they do not waste assets on the primary blockchain

The Flippening – Expected to happen in the future, when the market cap for Ethereum goes past that of Bitcoin, which would make Ethereum the single most valuable cryptocurrency of all time.

Token – What allows for decentralized and open source networks to be created and also incentives for people to take part in the network. Tokens have been made more popular through Ethereum and now there are many token networks in existence

Total Supply – The total amount of tokens or coins that exist for a specified digital asset. This includes those already in circulation as well as any that have been reserved or locked onto the network

Trading Volume – The total traded cryptocurrency during a specified time period

Transaction Block – A group of transactions that have been certified and pulled into a block. These transactions are then hashed, and the block added to the end of the blockchain

Transaction Fee – Every transaction carried out with cryptocurrency attracts a small fee. The miner for each block receive a percentage of the total block fees as their reward

Turing Complete – A machine that is capable of computing anything that needs to be computed. If any other programmable machine can compute it, the Turing Complete machine can also compute it. The EVM is an example of this.

Vitalik Buterin - One of the founders of the Ethereum network and the most well-known one.

Volatility – This refers to the movements of the price of a currency, recorded over a set period of time, A high volatility means that the price is unstable and, although it may rise fast, it can also crash hard without warning

W-Z

Wallet – A software or hardware solution for the storage of private cryptographic keys. These include software clients that let a user view their transactions and create new ones on the blockchain that the wallet is meant for. Most wallets are tied to being used on one blockchain only, for example, Bitcoin or Ethereum.

Wei – The smallest known Ether denomination, 1000000000000000000 Wei is equal to 1 Ether

Whale –An individual or group who own sufficient capital to conduct massive orders that may be used for market manipulation

Whitelist- A list of participants who have been approved and registered to take part in an ICO or in a Pre-Sale

Whitepaper – A document that is released prior to a project. The best known is the Bitcoin whitepaper that was released the year before Bitcoin and explained what it was all about and what its objectives were

Wire Transfer – A method of sending funds electronically from one person to another, often used as a way of getting fiat currency back from an exchange

Zerocoin – A new project with the goal of introducing real anonymity to Bitcoin network.

Zero Confirmation Transaction – A transaction made on the Bitcoin network that has been sent out to the nodes but is awaiting processing into a block Sometimes termed as unconfirmed transactions

References

http://blog.julioruiz.net

https://steemit.com

https://crushcrypto.com

https://cryptominded.com

https://blockgeeks.com

Conclusion

We all know that Bitcoin was the very first cryptocurrency and it remains at the top today. However, we all know that it is by no means the last, given the sheer number that has followed it and no doubt at some point, one or more of the others will topple it from its number one position.

Many of those that followed have built on what Bitcoin offered, improving on the fundamental concepts and offering richer features and a lot more functionality, not to mention speed. Darkcoin is offering anonymity while quark offers speed and security. Ghostcoin offers us a lightweight platform that won't eat up your resources while Huntercoin is offering an experience that is built on a game. Ethereum offers the smart contract while OmiseGO offers a system that bridges wallets and exchanges to make payments and transactions much faster and easier. Some are attempting to compete directly with Bitcoin while others offer a complimentary service. Any one of these and the hundreds of others has the potential to be the next Bitcoin or they could just crash and burn out of existence.

The real beauty of cryptocurrency lies in the way it lets users control their own money, make much faster transactions across the world, with fewer fees than traditional transfers. Provided they are used properly, any one of these digital currencies will serve the purpose it was developed for and no doubt many of them, like Bitcoin, will become the foundation for the next generation of cryptocurrencies as developer seek to find better uses for the blockchain, faster and more efficient ways of making transactions and more secure ways of allowing us to become our own bankers.

Thank you for taking the time to read my guide; I hope that you found it helpful and that I have managed to answer any questions you may have had. All that remains now is for you to determine whether you are brave enough to make the jump.

About the Author

Jack Monroe is a Cryptocurrency specialist, Entrepreneur and Author of numerous books to help others with growth and development. As an early Entrepreneur, his focus has switched towards Cryptocurrency investment. Trading, Mining and investing in Bitcoin, Ethereum, Litecoin, Ripple, Ethos, and other Altcoins has given Jack a future and the knowledge to provide valuable skills and training to others in the world of Cryptocurrency.

Jack Monroe is a family man who only aspires to build a strong foundation for his family. He believes that with hard work and mindfulness, success and abundance will come. With his accomplishments, Jack chose to help others understand that Successful Investing is about managing risk, not avoiding it.